Treasures of Darkness

Treasures of Darkness

Ken Hekman

Writers Club Press
San Jose New York Lincoln Shanghai

Treasures of Darkness

Writers Club Press
an imprint of iUniverse.com, Inc.

For information address:
iUniverse.com, Inc.
5220 S 16th, Ste. 200
Lincoln, NE 68512
www.iuniverse.com

ISBN: 0-595-18179-1

Printed in the United States of America

To the memory of Carla, who made us so much better than we would have been without her.

To Mike

Thanks for caring

Ken Held

"I will give you the treasures of darkness, riches stored in secret places, so that you will know that I am the Lord, the God of Israel, who summons you by name."

Isaiah 45:3

"Poetry is a language that tells us, through a more or less emotional reaction, something that cannot be said."

Edwin Arlington Robinson

Contents

Preface

Grief can be a very dangerous place. Personalities can change in the wake of grief, shattering relationships with the living, permanently altering motivations, instilling fear that defies consolation, and challenging every belief that you counted on to sustain you in tough times. Sorrow can easily be compounded when marriages fall apart or when surviving children can no longer find the love of their parents. Grieving families are at risk for a host of physical, spiritual and emotional challenges, any one of which can be sufficient to destroy what remains of fragile relationships.

But grief can also bear extraordinary rewards. There is a freedom that comes from facing death head on unlike any other freedom known to man. There are insights and perspectives about ourselves, about life, about God, and about relationships, that jump off the page in the book of grief. I've tried to capture a few of those treasures in these writings, but my ambition for the reader goes beyond gaining the gems of my journey. I hope that you can use what you learn to find your own gems, to face your own sorrow—whatever its source and character—to glean profound lessons that benefit you and those around you.

I present this journey through four stages. We all start out afraid to die. We can profess to look forward to eternal life, but until we stare death in the face, we're all afraid of it. The next stage began for me the moment I heard of Carla's death. I was afraid to live—and to love—again. That fear led me over several months to a third place. I was no longer afraid to die. I would have welcomed it. The fourth stage began to emerge for me after a few years. That's where I am most of the time now—not afraid to live, and to love, again.

Afraid to Die

We were a charmed family.

We were characterized by love, by health, by all the trappings of middle-class Americans. We were unusual in that we were still happily married after more than twenty years, and that all three of our kids were developing as responsible, talented and likeable people. We even had the benefit of a traditional family life, where Dad was the sole breadwinner and Mom was able to devote her time to keeping the household, a little volunteer work and her natural artistic abilities. We had a nice home, a couple of decent cars, took memorable vacations together, and generally enjoyed life as we knew it. We were pretty normal by anyone's definition.

In that context, I had grown accustomed to feeling fortunate. I had enjoyed a progressive career in health care, leading to my current role as an independent consultant for medical practices nationwide. I had been successful in business, in love, in friendships, and even in writing, with my first business book published just two years before our loss. I had reason to believe that I had some degree of control over my destiny, and that my future destiny was going to be as charmed as my past. I was in the midst of writing my second book, and had ambitions as a health care reformer with an international presence. I was confident that with perseverance and strategic contacts, I could make it happen.

When everything's going your way, death seems pretty remote. As a Christian, I knew what I needed to know about death. I knew that it was a necessary means of entering heaven. I knew that I had nothing to fear in death because I was committed to the Lord, had accepted the free gift of salvation, and that He was preparing a place for *me*. I was as ready for death as I thought I needed to be. I had made my will and purchased the right insurance policy to protect my family, and I had a belief system to protect my soul.

We had also prepared our family for death in the same way, teaching them to be ready to meet their Maker at any time by trusting in Him for everything. We were active in church. All three kids went to Christian schools, as my wife and I had when we were growing up. Our faith was alive.

But as I look back, I have to acknowledge that we still feared death profoundly. We could say we were not afraid to die because we knew we would go to heaven, but knowing it didn't mean we could face it without great fear. We planned guardians if we both were taken at the same time, and worried about our kids when they traveled, just like most parents. But the eventuality was so remote, so unthinkable, so detestable, that it left my mind as soon as it entered.

I guess I also thought that being Christians gave us some sort of protection—like God would never let us encounter something we couldn't handle. I understood my loving family to be an extension of God's love, and fully expected that neither He nor my family would ever interrupt that love. Being a Christian meant we were safe—by my understanding of the term.

I was naïve.

It's ironic now as I look back. My assumption of safety, of special protection from God, lulled me into believing that death was not to be feared, when in fact I feared death more than I knew. I could pretend to not fear it because I hadn't really faced it, but all pretension melted away when I had to deal with the real thing. Then I found out how much I really had feared it all along.

So that was the first part of my journey—years and years of quiet assumptions about faith being sufficient in all things, but without really having to put that faith to the test. I had lived decades of being ready to die (in my head), without having to feel the heat of it in my heart. The fact of the matter was, I was afraid to die.

All that changed in an instant.

Carla was so full of life. To know her was to love her. With blond hair, brown eyes and the warmest smile, she could charm anyone's heart. She was the first of our three children. She was a senior at Holland Christian High School, looking forward to college in the fall. She was on the springboard of her life, ready to dive in with enthusiastic optimism.

She was an excellent student with special interests in creative writing, Spanish and the arts. She loved doing things with her family as well as her friends. Her sister, Jill, three years younger, was becoming a best friend, and Dan, eight years her junior, looked up to Carla as a model of teenage maturity. Her friends were the kinds of kids all parents would be proud of. She took frequent walks in the evening, usually with her mom, and looked forward to nights out with her dad. She was naturally affectionate, and invariably kissed her parents goodnight before heading for bed. She had her share of typical (but minor) teenage struggles, but by and large, Carla was a wonderful daughter.

On January 9, 1998, Carla Hekman's life on earth came to an end. She was on her way to a function at the high school when her car hit a patch of ice and slid into the path of an oncoming vehicle. The impact on the passenger side of her car caused fatal injuries to her head and neck. She died instantly. She was alone in the car. No one in the other vehicle was injured. Both cars were traveling under the speed limit. All were wearing seat belts and no alcohol was involved. She was 17.

By all human understanding, it was an accident.

Afraid to Live

Every Parent's Nightmare

Where can I begin again?

Death is life-shattering. The pieces are strewn about, without order, and spattered with painful tears. The natural order has been disrupted in a most grievous way. Kids aren't supposed to die before their parents, especially good kids. She didn't deserve this. We didn't deserve this.

It's been a week of horror. First, Jill burst into our bedroom with those dreaded words, "The sheriff is at the door!" Then after throwing on a cover, hoping to dodge the inevitable, we were told to sit down.

"Your daughter, Carla, has been in an accident tonight," he said. "Her car went out of control on an icy road, and she was broad-sided by another vehicle. She was taken to the Emergency Room at Holland Hospital where she was pronounced dead." He handed us her purse and her picture ID. It was Carla. "I want to extend my condolences. I'm very sorry."

A primal scream rose within me, but only a painful groan came out. Marybeth cried "Oh no!" and became pale with pain. We hugged in an effort to drive away the truth. Jill joined us, shaking and weeping. I was too stunned to cry just then. I wanted to, but the horror of the moment was too vivid for tears.

The deputy offered to call someone for us - a pastor, a family member. I stood and wandered toward the kitchen. He pulled me aside. "Sir, you or someone from your family will have to go to the hospital...to identify the body." I completed the sentence for him. I knew the procedure. I'd watched enough TV. I'd been trained as an emergency medical technician and had been a first responder many times. But this wasn't fiction, and it wasn't someone else's flesh and blood. This was mine. This tragedy was personal.

I agreed to let the deputies call our pastor. I found the directory, but my hands shook so badly I couldn't read it or flip the pages with my normal dexterity. Nothing was normal. I told the deputy to look for Rev. Jim Boer and handed the directory to him. He dialed. No answer.

I couldn't fasten the seat belt in the patrol car. One of the officers buckled me safely in. The car was warm, but I wasn't. I felt cold from somewhere deep inside. The coldness refused to be warmed, and it became my companion for months. We drove an alternate route to the hospital. The accident happened on the road we always traveled toward town. It was on the way to everything. We stopped at Jim Boer's house first. The officers woke him from a deep sleep. I watched from the car as they explained their intrusion. He doubled over with pain. A moment later we were driving the final mile toward the hospital where Jim would meet me.

I was escorted to a small waiting room off the entrance to the ER. The doctor explained what he knew - massive head injuries, bled from her ears, no responsiveness in the field or in the emergency room, probably died instantly, will want to do an autopsy, still has an endo-tracheal tube. I'd heard too much already. As a social worker and I left the shelter of the cozy waiting area and headed for the dreaded room, Jim Boer was waiting for me, shaking his head. He hugged me tight. It helped, but it didn't change anything.

I felt the sorrowful faces of a dozen staff in hospital scrubs, mirroring the pain in my own face. All the doors to the treatment rooms I could see were open, except one. It had a tall, narrow window pane, opaque except for a two-inch strip in the middle. I approached the door. I caught my first glimpse of her through that strip of clear window pane. I knew immediately. She was gone.

The horror of the next few minutes tore my heart and left it permanently scarred. *My* daughter, so full of life such a short time ago, was now so full of death, so pale and breathless. I touched her hand and was shocked by its coolness. The useless tube in her mouth distorted her face, and her eyes—those beautiful brown eyes—stared into nothingness. The lifeless form stretched before me was too much to bear. I cried out in agony, collapsed to my knees, and begged to be taken away. I had seen too much. I had become old so quickly. I was trapped in every parent's worst nightmare.

Jim and I left under our own feeble power. I searched for a water fountain. I had never been so thirsty. Water would feed my soul, I hoped. It moistened my throat, but my soul still thirsted. "This is about the sovereignty of God," I told Jim as we walked out into the stinging cold. "It is too perfect. She died instantly. The car was struck on the passenger side. No one is to blame. God just took her." We walked to Jim's van and got in, unable to speak any more. He took me home, past the site of the accident. I could see marks in the snow, but little else. We did not stop. Maybe she was driving a little too fast for the conditions, I wondered aloud. "Don't even think it," Jim replied.

God took her. She walked with God and God took her. Just like Enoch.

By morning, it was time for phone calls, starting with my parents, who had already lost two other grandchildren. "It's Carla," I said. "She was killed in a car accident last night, just a few hours ago." The agony in my soul echoed 2,000 miles away over the phone line. It was a scene to be repeated by a dozen more calls to family members around the continent. I wanted to talk to each one myself. I wanted to hear the voices of my brothers and sisters and my in-laws. It was as though I needed their love and companionship desperately. I knew they would scream in agony when I inflicted those horrible words, but I also knew that the agonizing cries would somehow bring comfort to my deep, deep wounds. The details began to flow like a script, but the pain was freshened with each conversation.

By mid-morning, the world knew the horror in our hearts. Family and friends began to come over. Some with food, many with tears, all with deep, deep sadness. We put her picture on the mantle. I placed a draft of a poem about Carla Roo that came to me in the sleepless night. The day turned into a blur of people coming and going.

The next five days seemed like they contained more pain than any single lifetime ought to endure. The unthinkable grew undeniable. The permanence, the finality of it all was so thunderous. There was no escape, no chance for negotiated peace. Every moment, whether asleep or awake, was overwhelmingly contaminated with pain.

But there were things to do, people to see.

The details of housing for out-of-town guests fell to others. Food arrived for our physical sustenance, but far beyond our appetites. Within hours of daybreak, Marybeth and I were meeting with a funeral director, making decisions we considered unimaginable just the day before. All the while, the vacuum in our hearts grew to numbing proportion, though we wanted desperately to fill it, and family and friends wanted to do anything to help us. What we all wanted most for each other, we were powerless to give. Only Carla's presence could fill this gaping hole, and that was not to be.

Somehow, schedules took over. We answered the phone when it rang, opened the door when people knocked, and showed up when and where we were told to by the funeral director. We met with the family of the people in the other car, trying to comfort them as they tried to comfort us. News people called for interviews, which I readily granted in a feeble attempt to tell the story of Carla's wonderful life, and our desperate search for meaning began. These were not schedules we would choose, but somehow they became keys to survival. Perhaps we were too weak to think for ourselves, and the tasks placed before us enabled us to put one foot ahead of the other. Response was easy. Initiation was impossible.

But at the same time, each response we chose seemed a welcome contrast to the out-of-control sense that overwhelmed us. I imagined that I was choosing to answer the phone when it rang, grasping desperately for something I could be in charge of once again. I carefully selected words to use in response to agonized comments like an editor might compose headlines for the leading stories. Feigned confidence seemed to be the only tool, mythical as it was, to fight the inimitable dragon called Death.

Time had always seemed friendly to us, but now it was our enemy. We had aged gracefully, one day at a time, until now. I found myself longing for each of those single days to have lasted longer, to prolong forever the inevitability of the present moments. As much as I longed for the past, I dreaded the future. The fear of the unknown screamed at remembered love, drowning its gentle voice for what seemed like eternity.

Then came the time to go to the funeral home as a family for our first view of Carla in a casket.

There is something simultaneously dreadful and comforting about seeing someone you love in a casket. The sting of death attacks with merciless ferocity, but it only touches those outside the box. The agony of our own distress shrieked in contrast to the peaceful appearance of a body at rest. Our pain was just beginning. Hers was over. Anguish was mixed with jealousy. If I were in her place, my loss would be a memory rather than the ever-present knowledge at the core of my soul that this loss is humanly permanent.

It was time for tears. The numbness subsided just enough to feel the pain in all its rawness. Sobs weren't enough. Nothing short of wailing would do, but with it came a strange satisfaction. I cried until I could cry no more. It changed nothing, of course, but when the wailing came to a natural end, it seemed to signal, in the smallest of ways, hope for a measure of peace. I found, for a moment, a foothold at the bottom of the pit.

We consented to have her close friends visit the funeral home as a separate group the day before the public visitation. Their loss was distinct from ours, but equally profound. They still had their hopes and dreams before them, damaged to be sure, but present nonetheless. Feelings of loss placed a permanent exclamation mark on fears of their own mortality. Here they were, at the height of their carefree, invulnerable youth, slapped in the face in a most grievous way with the ugly truth about just how vulnerable they are. They weren't kids anymore.

They had been so much a part of our lives, staying overnight, going on vacations with us, participating in the family banter around our kitchen table. They were a part of us, not in the same way Carla was, of course, but they enriched our lives in a unique way. And now we would be inextricably entwined with them, but not in the ways we thought. They would go to college, maturing and fulfilling their hopes and dreams. Would we be able to enjoy them as we watched them grow? Would we cheer their accomplishments, celebrate their weddings, marvel at their children in the same way? Or would every encounter be tinged with sadness and jealousy for what might have been?

We braced ourselves for that most Midwest of traditions, the visitation. The day before the funeral, we met over 800 visitors in four hours at the funeral home. People came from deep in our past to be near to our hearts. Platitudes were spoken, but mostly I remember the look in the eyes of hundreds of friends. It was a look that ran forty miles deep. It mirrored the look in my own eyes. It told me they felt what they could not express in words. We hugged a lot, told short stories about Carla, resisted longer conversations for the sake of the growing line of visitors, and stood by the coffin surrounded by massive bouquets from around the country.

The crowd at the funeral was at least 10% more than the church's capacity, but everyone had a reason to be there. It was a time of pain and grace. The storytellers gave a balanced picture of their dear friend, including a quip

14

about Carla's spontaneity with an ice cream cone (smashing it in her friend's face). Her boss talked about her excellent work and announced a new award for employees who would exemplify her. The sermon was one-of-a-kind, delivered by a one-of-a-kind friend - Jim Boer, the pastor who had been with me in the Emergency Department. Carla was cast as the Conqueror. This quiet, fun-loving, unassuming teenager showed us all how to overcome the deadliest force of all, the force of evil. Her simple faith and submission to her Lord spoke volumes. She was an angel among us, and we didn't know it.

The visitation and the funeral overwhelmed us. The number of people, the intensity of their feelings for us—it all seemed too much to bear. I somehow felt responsible for their grief, and wanted to comfort others more than I wanted to be comforted. At least I had a sense of how to comfort others. I was a complete novice at being comforted, at least for something as tragic as this.

The chill in the air (14 degrees F) matched the chill in our hearts as we laid her to rest at the cemetery. We didn't linger. There would be time for that later.

The joy of watching our children grow seemed to have come to an abrupt end. We knew that we would think of life in two segments - before and after. We would still watch Jill and Dan grow, if God willed it, but always with a measure of fear mixed with the love. Pure joy was a thing of the past. Only impure joy - cautious hope - remained. The normal risks of having children seemed academic in the past, but they were terrifyingly real now. Would we ever dare to love them again in the same way? How would we deal with teenage emancipation?

Jill had lost her best friend, and she tried to cope by surrounding herself with other friends. She needed to have a taste of normalcy in the midst of this tragedy. Dan had to play to cope. He needed to feel like a kid again, to prove to himself that he was still alive. Marybeth spent hours putting him to bed at night, holding him, rubbing his back, talking in her most soothing voice. Dan wanted to know the details of the accident and the rescue attempt. Jill didn't.

We began to get a taste of how our loss of Carla would change our family relationships forever. We didn't know—couldn't know—the significance at the time, but the middle child was no longer the middle child. Instead of two girls and one boy, we now had one of each gender. We began to see how Carla's presence shaped all other relationships, and how her absence put each of us in a different light.

I affectionately called my daughter Carla Roo, a play on her middle name and characters from Winnie the Pooh. The name began when she was a little girl, and stayed with her as she grew into a young woman.

Carla Roo

The meaning of your life is clear:
Your ready smile, your voice of cheer,
Your frequent hugs, the playful way
You graced our family every day
Your love of life warmed newcomers too.
You were a gift my Carla Roo.

The meaning of your death is dim.
And as we face this time so grim,
We cling to memories of love
And know you're with your Father above.
So now we say goodbye to you.
We love you dearly Carla Roo.

Spelunkers

We are spelunkers in the Mammoth Cave of Grief. It has been over 100 years since Mammoth Cave was discovered in Kentucky, but only a portion of it has been explored. That's what grief feels like to us. We may live a long time and still only explore a small part of this dark and dangerous place. We feel our way along with only the light of a candle that sometimes illuminates and sometimes flickers. And sometimes it goes out, but we are usually powerless to re-light it. It casts shadows on all but the closest parts of the cave, and cannot begin to penetrate the depth or breadth of the cavern in a single glow. Parts of it have been explored before, but this is the first time we have been here. Other parts may have never been explored, or there are no records of exploration. We find ourselves in tight spots with regularity, and frequently need to be rescued by friends. Sometimes we are at the end of our rope, and the ropes seem frayed, compounding our danger. Around every corner there are new caverns to explore, some more frightening than others. Each loss we have ever endured is marked by another branch, another room of the grand cavern. We seem trapped in this place, unable to emerge until we have explored it all. It is always cold here, and we are always covered from head to toe with the dust and filth of our surroundings. It is futile and painful for someone to tell us to leave the cave (to "get over it"). It only accentuates our entrapment.

There is one vital resource, however, that is common to every part of the cave. Air. Every respiration is an inspiration to go on. Air is everywhere, like God is in every part of our Cavern of Grief. He did not put us here, and we did not go here on purpose. We fell in and the opening was closed around us. But we will not suffocate.

Sometimes each family member is in a different room of the cave. Sometimes we're in the same room, but even then, we see our surroundings differently. Marybeth's birthday came and went, but it was not happy. I told her I wished her many more birthdays, but I realize that I want them for myself more than for her. The thought of losing another loved one is unbearable, but the thought of dying is not.

Do not pray that we will emerge from the Mammoth Cave of Grief until our work is done here. Pray instead that we will have the courage to go on. Pray that we will have the strength to explore a little more each day and that we will be enriched by what we find. Pray that we will have sufficient supplies to stay as long as we need to, and that the air will always be fresh. Pray that our lights will burn brighter and that the air will reflect and expand the glow, illuminating even the hard-to-find treasures that lie hidden here. Pray that we will be able to chart our course and record it in such a way that others who follow us will make it through this cave safely and will learn to appreciate its nuances. Pray that we will become confident and well-equipped to be tour guides.

Pray for us, but pray also for yourselves. Pray that you will be able to learn from our journey. Pray that you will find the right ways to support us from above ground. Pray that you might find valuable questions to ask us about our experience, as we are going through it, so that you too may be enriched by our findings without having to go here yourselves. I promise to answer your questions and not be offended by them. Do not try to protect us from the darkness of the cave by avoiding questions that may evoke fresh pain. Your questions may lead us into new and previously unexplored chambers, revealing treasures of enormous value.

Keep praying.

Mourning on Purpose

The gray tomorrows refuse to fade
Revealing a brighter dawn.
They blend with the fog of yesterday
To moisten my eyes some more.

I live in the shadows now.

The clocks and the cars keep rhythm alive
Pretending that I can go on.
Well-meaning advisors speak nonsense to me
Of moving beyond the door.

I live in the shadows now.

I'm mourning on purpose, so let me be
A slave to the cavernous yawn.
I'm mining for wisdom and wish to stay
Where I've never been before.

I live in the shadows now.

Dream

I woke up this morning during a dream. I don't remember the theme of the dream, but all I remember is that Carla appeared at the end. She just looked at me from behind a kitchen counter and smiled. I gasped. I said, "You're back! How are you?" Even as I said the words, I knew it was a dream. It just seemed so real. But she never answered. Her smile and her eyes did all the speaking. They seemed to say, "I'm fine, Dad, and you can be too. I understand everything now and I'm fine." She looked deeply contented—a masterwork of peace. My dream ended. Is this a cruel hoax or a heavenly messenger? My heart aches again. She was so close, yet so far.

Holding Up

How are we doing? That's the question we hear most often of course. The other day someone asked how Marybeth was "holding up." I thought it a strange question, although it's not. Part of me wanted to scream, "Can't you see we are legless? There is no 'holding up.' There is only 'being held up.'" Faith, if it was worth anything, would have to come from outside ourselves.

That faith became palpable one day after a meeting at church. I felt extraordinarily heavy. As I walked across the parking lot to my car, I felt a supernatural sensation. It was as though my legs were not my own. They were young and strong and vital, and they seemed to carry my body. In that moment, it was as though Jesus' legs were a welcome substitute for my own weary underpinnings. I felt wise, even though my sensation was more physical than intellectual or emotional. My legs tingled, and my heart sang with gratitude.

Sovereignty

I think a lot about the sovereignty, the supremacy of God. I memorized the card that told us to find comfort in it, but sometimes my heart of hearts knows that there was lost potential and purpose unaccomplished. My sorrow deepens. I am terrified of this supreme God. Comfort seems like the last thing I would go to him for. How can this be love? It feels like the antithesis of love. What did I do to deserve this? Am I guilty beyond my peers? Sovereignty is more terrifying than comforting. If the fear of the Lord comes before wisdom, then please Lord, hurry up and make me wise. The heat of the burning bush is scorching my soul.

I thought trusting a sovereign God meant that I had some sort of special protection. He shields me from the wages of sin, but here I am smitten by death anyway. I thought we had a deal, but now I know that I didn't understand all the terms. I signed on without reading the fine print. I loved Carla freely as only a father can. I had vibrant hopes for her. She had hopes too. Love conquers all, right?

I need a new deal with God. I need to understand him in a different way. I need to see what he meant by the fine print. I feel a little like I am an entrepreneur in a foreign land, trying to negotiate a deal in their language. I'm at a distinct disadvantage. God holds all the cards.

Purple Was Her Color

Purple was her color.
It gave her great delight
She chose it for her room and
She wore it banquet night.

I called her May Day Princess
For that's when she was born.
Her royal flair came early
When dress-up clothes were worn.

And as she grew she broadened
Her taste for different hues.
Her favorite from the rainbow
Was difficult to choose.

To capture every mood,
Sometimes she'd wear them all.
Her favorite tie-dye shirt
Matched nothing but her soul.

Her purple sweater was
The Christmas gift we gave.
But we did not know then
She'd wear it to her grave.

But purple was her color.
No need to change a thing.
That sweater was just right
For her to meet the King.

I Need A Bigger God
A conversation with God

I need a bigger God
Than what I had before.
I thought he was enough
But now I need him more.

A weekend God was fine
When things were going well.
But Sundays just don't last
When you're in living hell.

I need a bigger God
Who's been where I have been.
Someone who suffered hard
And lived to hope again.

"I AM THE GREAT I AM.
The one who made the earth.
And from the dawn of time,
I planned your very birth.

The universe so vast
Can fit inside my hand.
So many things I know
You cannot understand.

And when creation fell
I made another way
To bring you back to me.
But what a price to pay!

Can you just trust me now
For things I cannot show?
I love you so much more
Than you will ever know."

I thank you Sovereign Lord
For giving me your view,
Revealing holiness
Much greater than I knew.

Forgive me Son of God
For being so unwise.
Please live in me as though
You are uncompromised.

Pity

Among all the feelings
That torture my soul,
Self-pity's free-wheelings
Extract a great toll.

The quicksand of sorrow
Can subtly lay claim
To hopes of tomorrow
And yesterday's fame.

A wasted emotion,
Self-pity must be.
What drives this devotion
To care just for me?

But pity is part of the
Grief that we feel,
Like blood cleans a cut
And helps it to heal.

To look for its value
And reap its reward,
Just take it in stride while you
Reach for the Lord.

Forever Sad

I shall be forever sad
And mourn the loss of love I had,
For though I try, I cannot hide
The anguish that I feel inside.

This look of pain will never fade.
My furrowed brow must ever shade
The piercing view of haunted eyes
That saw too much to be disguised.

The corners of my mouth turn down
As though a monumental frown
Has now displaced a thousand smiles
And left distortion to beguile.

So as you gaze on Sorrow's face,
Take time to leave a warm embrace,
Or ponder as you pass me by,
"There, but for God's grace...(*go I?*)"

Family Grief

We understand that the death of a child can be traumatic to a marriage. Marybeth and I enjoy a strong and vital marriage, but I'm sure that any union can be placed at risk if the two follow different paths in grief as in life. We can't take anything for granted.

Our present journey began with the shared experience of the sheriff deputies in our living room. Every parent's nightmare was our joint nightmare. But our experiences followed different paths right after that. I went with the deputies to the hospital to identify Carla's body. Rev. Jim Boer met me there. Marybeth stayed home. A week later, my brother and I went to dispose of the car. Marybeth stayed home. I'm glad she wasn't a part of two of my three traumatic moments. Seeing the body in the casket for the first time was very traumatic for her. I wept bitterly too, but I was relieved that Carla looked so much better than she did in the emergency room.

We are each grieving more than the loss of our daughter too. Marybeth lost a good friend and walking mate. I lost an immeasurable amount of personal power in the recognition that I cannot protect my family from human pain and misery. We both hurt for Jill and Dan as we watch them grieve the Carla they each knew; and we know that the hole in their respective lives from the loss of Carla is different from the hole in our lives.

I find value in connecting with a lot of people by phone, by e-mail, and by visits. Marybeth wants to connect with only a few. So we've set some boundaries. We don't make any commitments for each other without checking first. I draft "Dear All" e-mail messages and she edits them before they go out. She has allowed me time to read which I find helpful. I have allowed her time to paint which she finds helpful.

Throughout our twenty-plus years together, we have often set aside time to talk an hour or so before we go to bed. We now talk frequently during the day as well. We began the day after the funeral with a little routine. It took a whole day to read the cards and letters we had received to that point. We continued with our daily ritual of opening cards together after the mail arrived for the next several weeks. We read them together, then talked about the people that sent them, and made connections with other cards, or other people, and relished our time together.

We grieve as we live: I am more analytical, verbose, and driven; she is more reflective and private. But we talk openly about our feelings of the day and the experiences we have together and separately. Sometimes I'll quantify my feeling as a value between one and ten, and sometimes she'll respond with a value of her own. We grieve at different paces and different places, but we understand that difference, and are willing to give each other the space we need.

Perhaps most important, though, is that we are determined to not be defeated by this experience. We love each other dearly, and all the more so as we realize how precious life is. We are dedicated to grow in love and to nurture Jill and Dan as fully as we nurtured Carla. We feel privileged to have been Carla's parents. It was an honor to have such a wonderful daughter for the time we had her. We've been enriched by the chance to love her and to be loved by her. We are so thankful we invested fully in her and in Jill and Dan. We are so grateful for the life we had together, the vacations, the holidays, the traditions, the routines. Every piece of our life with Carla was delicious. We are determined to savor those memories, and to build new memories together with Jill and Dan and with all our loved ones.

No Guarantees

When kids are born to families
Where love is clearly felt,
The world seems right and we are pleased
With cards just as they're dealt.

But when we see a tragedy
Disrupt our gentle flow,
We're quick to point accusingly
And ask about God's role.

But we're not told his mysteries
And he need not explain.
For God gives us no guarantees
Of life that's free of pain.

Him Alone

When God reveals his deepest truth
He sometimes uses means
That overwhelm and flood our souls.
He draws us in to lean
On him alone.

His scorching sovereignty
Brings self-deception to its knees.
It strips us of our arrogance,
Extracting humble pleas
For him alone.

We're vulnerable before his face
And ready to receive
The blessings kept for those who mourn,
For those who still believe
In him alone.

Wrestling with God

I wrestle with God but it seems he's not there.
I lunge at his throat but I only grasp air.

I'm raging at him for causing my grief
So why do I seek him when I need relief?

Can God whose lowest blow takes my breath
Be the same one who knows and cares about death?

His silence like punishment won't satisfy
My hunger for comfort. I keep asking "Why?"

The anguish consumes me. I'm left in despair.
My hope has run out. Face me God if you dare!

Where's grace when I need it, I'm begging you Lord.
I must have your answers! I won't be ignored!

Emptiness

I never knew emptiness felt like this,
A cavern so dreadful, an endless abyss;
A tunnel so dark it hems me in
With silence so deafening amidst the din.
How deep is the sadness of broken ties.
The answers are absent to thousands of "Whys?"
I never imagined what I might miss,
For who could know emptiness felt like this.

It Hurts to be Human

It hurts to be human,
It's painful to know
The love and the grief
In the soul of my soul.

It hurts to be human,
To come to the rim
Of Hope's invitation
And still not go in.

It hurts to be human,
To try and to fail,
To reach for the ring
But to no avail.

It hurts to be human,
To know all too well,
That searching for heaven
Can lead us through hell.

It hurts to be human,
So God, if you please,
I'll thank you to free me
From human disease.

It hurts to be human,
So do what you can
To lighten the spirit
Of this painful man.

It hurts to be human.
I long for the day
When Christ will return
To chase pain away.

It hurts to be human
To give birth to one
Who laughs like a brook,
And shines like the sun.

It hurts to be human,
But thanks just the same.
For as she was growing
You called her by name.

It hurts to be human,
But through all these tears,
I'm grateful we had her
For seventeen years.

Grief Is The Price You Pay For Love

Grief is the price you pay for love
Like night repays the day.
It hovers like a cloud above,
But never goes away.

It seizes memories beloved
And colors them in gray;
It steals the hopes you're dreaming of
And seals them all to stay.

Affection never is enough
To fill our lives the way
We want it to when all's rebuffed,
And we are left to pray.

Shock

Traumatic separation is
An exponential shock,
When hope, one moment bright, becomes,
The next, a keyless lock.

I grasp, at best, with slippery fingers;
Yet, I can't let go.
My heart refuses to accept
The truth my head must know:

How quickly life can change for ill,
How swiftly it can pass.
When optimistic dreams return
A hoax in deep morass.

The Star

Today we got pictures developed from before she died. One of them shows her with her arm around my neck, reaching for the top of the Christmas tree with a star in her hand, ready to put on the crown. We're both looking at the star, straining for it, and smiling. What a picture!

I remember that night, the Friday after Thanksgiving, when we decorated the tree. Carla didn't want to participate at first. She was a little grumpy, but gradually gave in and helped us when I asked her to put the star on top. So there she is, star in hand, reaching for the pinnacle of the lighted tree, arm around my shoulder, one foot in my hand-sling, reaching, reaching…

When I saw the picture, I cried hard. I visualized Carla, a stellar performer in her own rite, reaching prophetically for the Christmas Star, none of us aware that she would soon touch the Lord himself.

Sighing

Sighing comes easily
Like a sweet memory
That floods me with longing
Of things not to be.
It whispers of apathy,
Groans of my gravity,
And cries out for all to see
My soul's deepest "Ah me!"

Not Afraid to Die

Tears

I'm sure that others expect that I will not cry in public, but I am undeterred by their expectations. If I must avoid the public eye until my eyes are dry, I may never return. I will weep comfortably in any setting, because I must. If my behavior is labeled as "lost composure," I will pity those who do not understand, and educate them as I can. Composure is of limited value in my new world - the world stripped of pretense. I have found a new freedom to feel my feelings as they occur, and I am clear in understanding that this is as it should be. My goal is not to make others uncomfortable so much as to be true to myself, to be fully human. If they feel discomfort by my tears, I expect it is because they are unable or unwilling to face pain in their own lives.

Tears are cleansing. They seem to wash away the stain of pain, while at the same time signal to others that I have lost something or someone exceptionally dear to me. They bring relief while they also mark me. I think of them as my personal badge of courage. Tears speak to others of the wound they cannot see, and remind their hearts of the pain of the human experience we all hope to avoid.

Short of tears, I think I must startle people even with the look of pain in my face. I cannot control it even though I have tried. I know that it may reshape me forever, but I hope that a life of gratitude and hopefulness will chase the shadows around my eyes and the perpetual frown away.

Tears

Do not be ashamed of choosing to weep,
For tears are the blood of the soul.
It's sadder by far to see people keep
Their feelings from making them whole.

I Cry to the Sky

I cry to the sky as the day fades to night,
The hesitant tears finally give up their fight,
Remembering the daughter who drew me outdoors
With hiking and biking and camps by the shores.

A whippoorwill coos and a crow heads for home,
But anguish compels me to write one more poem.
The moon and the stars from their place beyond time
Encourage the rhythm and welcome the rhyme.

They call to my reason and sing to my soul,
And hint of their secrets to make my heart whole,
For they witnessed all that we learned as we grew:
That love can't be lost when it's proven so true.

First Things First

One thing I've learned through these events is that we've got it all backwards. We think our job as parents and teachers is to get our kids ready for careers and marriage and to be responsible citizens. We think our job is to help them succeed financially, to be independent. When we ask graduates, "What are you going to do after high school?" we're usually inquiring about how they're going to make their way in the world.

We've got it all wrong. We're so short-sighted. Our main job is to get them ready for heaven. The rest will come. Matthew was right. "Seek first the kingdom of God, and you'll get everything you need." If we put first things first, there is a better question we need to ask them. "**Who** are you going to be?" Or even better, "**Whose** are you going to be?" Answer that question first, and the rest will fall into place. The Who is more important than the What.

Forever Seventeen

Come visit me by dream tonight.
Return as though you still delight
My heart with hope of one more day
Of father-daughter interplay.

Pretend you need me to remind
You how to set your clock on time,
Or where to find your other shoe,
The way you often used to do.

Or have a seat and play a tune,
And take your time. Don't quit too soon,
For I could listen all night long
To every sweet familiar song.

Let's take a walk around the block,
Resume our simple idle talk
Of college plans and marriage hope.
(I might have paid you to elope.)

I must imagine just once more
You are my daughter like before.
You'll be forever seventeen,
But I still love, and I can dream.

Stars

The darkest nights reveal the farthest stars
Like diamonds in a cavern cold and deep.
The distant globes of massive brilliant flame
Are only seen by those who find no sleep.
While dreams consume most connoisseurs of life
My restless path remains exposed and steep.
For we who live in darkness know full well
The haunting awe a chilling night can keep.

An Act of God

What must we call a circumstance
When no one is to blame,
When trouble comes as if by chance
When lightning sparks a flame?

When human comprehension ends
Who then receives our nod?
The One on whom all life depends.
A random act of God.

But what about those other days
When hope shines undeterred,
When health and peace routinely stay,
Investments reap returns?

Are blessings any more deserved,
Now whom should we applaud?
But grace is also His to serve;
A random act of God.

What is Wisdom?

First Answer: I don't think a wise person can answer the question of what wisdom is. I thought I was somewhat wise before, but now I recognize my capacity as cleverness. Many clever people are not wise; and many wise people are not clever. I may still be clever, but whatever wisdom I may have possessed seems to have vanished.

Second Answer: Wisdom is what sticks to you when you encounter God. Many people are so slick that, even though they encounter God regularly, nothing sticks. Others may be ready to let wisdom stick, but they avoid encounters with God, or simply fail to recognize him in the routine experiences of every day. But an experience like the loss of my daughter has seared me so that all slickness has been torched away. I am laid bare, with no layers of slime or slick to protect me, and therefore I am ready to become wise. I only hope that the wisdom will adhere to me for the rest of my life.

Obedience seems to melt the slickness from the inside out. Wisdom can come without the trauma we have endured, but one must *will* the slickness away by heeding God's invitation for encounters with Him. Wisdom is not a possession of any human being. It is the voice of God expressed through obedient men and women. It is the voice, the face, the hands and the feet of God, placed in action as an act of willing submission to the eternal, supreme authority of heaven and earth.

Third answer: Wisdom is a spark from the collision of good and evil that ignites the human soul.

Wisdom

Wisdom is what sticks to us when we encounter God.
He humbles our pretension and He crumbles our facade.

His students find their teacher in the hardest parts of life.
He marks us as his own as does a shepherd with his knife.

To face the pain brings greatest gain: of that I'm almost sure.
For fire destroys the chaff in us, but gold becomes more pure.

Let Wisdom whisper to your soul. Accept no compromise,
For there's no greater treasure on the earth than to be wise.

God-shaped Grief

I read Job last night, the whole book in one sitting. Job was a whiner. He seems so preoccupied with his own righteousness while his friends seem so preoccupied with his apparent guilt. None of them were looking at who God is, but I think I can understand why. We try to define our pain in our own terms. We try to shape our grief with concepts we can grasp. But God shapes grief differently. He shapes it in timelessness and in sovereignty, neither of which are concepts we can begin to grasp. We have no point of reference to deal with these things, so we try to describe and understand them with our own points of reference. But our tools for referencing are inadequate. It's like trying to measure infinity with mathematics. It's like trying to measure the oceans with a measuring cup. It's like trying to weigh the Rockies with a bathroom scale. We can't do it in a lifetime. I think that's probably God's point. He wants us to conclude that we are unable, with our own tools, to fathom life and death, so that we simply rely on him, trust him to hold us through them.

These are hard lessons, because I am wired to dig deeper until I find satisfying answers to unanswerable questions and to articulate them in terms that I can understand and explain to others. To discover that words can't be found to contain God and deliver him to others is frustrating to my humanness. But to do so would be God-like, and would require me to give up my humanness. This dichotomy makes the uniqueness of Christ even more wonderful. He is both God and man. He can fathom God's plan while feeling and enduring human suffering. His articulation is the cross and the empty tomb. Pain and grace. Sorrow and love.

In John 16, Jesus tells his disciples that their grief will turn to joy. He is describing his resurrection, and he says in verses 22-24, "Now is your time of grief, but I will see you again and you will rejoice, and no one will take away your joy. In that day you will no longer ask me anything. I tell you the truth, my Father will give you whatever you ask in my name. Until now you have not asked for anything in my name. Ask and you will receive, and your joy will be complete." What is he saying is the path to complete joy? It's his resurrection, the empty tomb. It's relying on his victory over death and ours. It's planting our complete faith and confidence that we live in eternity with him, and that we have transcended time and the circumstances of our lives. That seems to be confirmed in verse 33. "I have told you these things, so that in me you may have peace. In this world you will have trouble, but take heart! I have overcome the world."

What are the implications for my life if I rely on the resurrection? How will it impact the way I spend my time and energy? I think that I do not need to fear life's trouble. I don't need to fear that other family members and loved ones will die. I don't need to fear that my needs on earth will go unmet. I can live in confidence that this isn't my destination or my destiny. This isn't my home. It's the place I am right now, but it's not home. Home is heaven. Carla is home. The rest of us are traveling, longing to be home. Home is where we won't ask any more questions. Home is where we let God be God. And we can do that because he overcame the world with his resurrection and the promise of our eternal life.

It leaves me with a longing for timelessness that can take the shape of apathy for the present. It makes me simply want to be translated as quickly and painlessly as Carla was. It makes me not want to be here much longer. But I sense that God has other ideas for me. As long as I live and breathe, I sense that he wants me to seek his wisdom, to articulate it and translate it for my own benefit as well as for others.

In Jesus' prayer in John 17, he makes several references to being unified with the Father, and of making his disciples, and all believers, one with himself and with the Father. I believe he speaks of integrity, the integration of life and faith, of pain and grace. That's the path to "the full measure of joy."

(verse 13) So that's part of what integrity means, learning to integrate sorrow into my routines, into all of life. It makes sense. People who have experienced deep pain have a credibility that others lack. A life without pain can't be trusted, for it has not been tested. It is like a blueprint that has not been built. It might look nice on paper, but the true test is whether it can weather a storm and still be beautiful.

But a life with pain has lost its innocence. Pain leaves a mark, perhaps like weathered cedar. It doesn't have the freshness it once had, but it demonstrates a deeper, more rugged, enduring quality. Perseverance lends credibility and stability to life. It adds ballast to our ship, allowing us to tread deeper waters. A life that incorporates the pain of sorrow exudes richness and a quality that stands out, that demands to be reckoned with. It demonstrates honesty that may be beyond the capacity of most. It touches the soul of those who are ready for wisdom, but is lost on those who prefer the innocence of life without pain.

Shake All the Wicked Away

Inspired by Job 38

Order the morning, order the dawn,
Order a luminous day.
Take the earth's edges firmly in hand,
Shake all the wicked away.

Sculpture the land and sculpture the sea,
Sculpture the awesome sky.
Marking dimensions, molding their form,
Matching the gleam in your eye.

Come to my rescue, come to my side,
Chase away fearsome haunts
Heal what you can and quicken my soul;
Hasten my renaissance.

Thine is the power, Thine is the throne,
Thine is the heavenly host.
Fill me with wisdom, holiness, love.
Only in Thee will I boast.

Terrible Anointing

I did a poetry reading in upstate New York while consulting with a Christian physician there. He arranged it at the home of friends in their small church fellowship. About 30 people were there for worship and poetry. The worship began with music, scripture reading and prayer as the spirit led. Then, just before the poetry was introduced, one of the leaders stood and spoke in tongues. It was a beautiful language, followed by a most articulate interpretation by another leader. The message essentially was, "I will teach you the lessons of sorrow so you will know my sorrow, and will worship me with new wisdom." I was awestruck by the experience, the beauty of it, the clear articulation of the interpretation, and the significance of the message.

I felt that God was affirming grief in a powerful way. It was as though he was saying, "I know you by name. I know where you are at every moment, and you are part of My Plan. Keep writing poetry, for I am making plans for it." I think of that moment as the "terrible anointing." Later, I shared the story of that experience with another grieving father who continues to minister through his grief two decades after losing his teenage son. He said, "Yes, it is a terrible anointing. But aren't they all?"

I also find a sense of great comfort in the terrible anointing. God knows my name. He's calling me to life again. He's showing me that he's at work in the world, and he's inviting me to join him.

Homesick for Heaven

I'm homesick for heaven,
A place only seen
With eyes of faith
And a heart that leans
Upon its creator.
This sense of yearning,
Of not belonging
Is fueled by thoughts
Of those gone before;
But magnified brighter
By tongues of fire.

There is no containing
A soul's desire.

Though most delight
To celebrate
This home away from home,
I'll set my sights
To be translated,
My heart unabated.
For life's overrated.

Go Ahead and Grieve

Go ahead and grieve.
List everything you've lost.
The shattered hopes and dreams,
The total dreadful cost.

Go ahead and grieve.
And take a year or two,
For no one else can know
Just what (s)he meant to you.

Go ahead and grieve
A lifetime if you must
Find friends to share your pain
The best you dare to trust.

Go ahead and grieve.
There is no perfect path,
For Death's tornado leaves
An awful aftermath.

Go ahead and grieve
But don't go on alone.
Let Jesus' gentle arms
Embrace you as his own.

Go ahead and grieve
There is no need to hide.
Take heart the Savior wept
When Mary's brother died.

Go ahead and grieve.
Remember as you cope
That God knows well your pain.
Let Him restore your hope.

What is Honest Suffering?

I think it means to acknowledge that this is the pits. I think it means to call depression what it is. It means to be transparent while still being respectful of the needs of others around me. If others have needs that are more important to them than my needs, I should not burden them with mine, nor do I need to be the fulfillment of their need. I should step aside to a place where my needs can be met, and let others meet their needs. It means being able to cry quietly in public without shame.

A gracious sufferer doesn't necessarily rely on grace 100% of the time. To do that would be to deny our humanity. A human sufferer is an inconsistent one. Some days are better than others. The path toward healing isn't straight. God may be there the whole time, but that doesn't mean his presence is felt all the time or that he only leads in clear or straight paths. I may be in his green pasture, but I'm wandering all around it, and some grass is bitter while other grass may be sweet.

Honest grief means not making excuses for God. It means being able to tell God I'm angry at him without feeling guilty, but knowing that he understands my anger and my pain. God lost his son too, but he got him back again. I have to wait to get my daughter back again. Time is the cruel barrier for me, but time doesn't exist for God.

This has shaken my view of the world and of God. The world is not safe, and since God is in charge, he may not be safe either. I see the fearsomeness of his sovereignty again. When I am free-falling, can God provide a safety net when it is he who saw fit to snatch the daughter I loved? If he can protect me, will he? If he loves me, why do I feel like a victim?

"Sorrow and Love flow mingled down." That's the description of Christ's sacrifice. It's like pain and grace. Is it possible that love without sorrow is incomplete? Is the image of childbirth a metaphor for the human condition? Pain and ecstasy are in the same event with intensity that has few rivals. I thought of my former life as rather ideal—all grace, little pain. Was I missing something? And what about those whose lives are characterized mostly by pain? It's easier to see how they are missing the fullness of life if they do not enjoy love, but perhaps they know a richness that we who embrace painless love have missed.

Salvation comes through pain. Sanctification comes through refinement. The refiner's fire isn't pleasant, but it converts iron ore to steel.

Celebrated Terror

I'm struck about how American culture celebrates controlled terror. TV and movies depict violence with regularity. Sports offer thrills that bring us to the edge of our seats. Football, hockey, car racing, downhill skiing and other high profile sports all are incredibly violent and dangerous, and they are eaten up by the American public. *Titanic* was a blockbuster movie. It's a love story in the setting of one of the world's greatest tragedies. How can we celebrate tragedy like this?

I think the answer comes in the mythical belief that we can control the terror. We know it's just a movie or just a game. We celebrate winners in a competitive ring. We get a little bit of the feeling of God knowing that the outcome will be OK. The movie will end on an upbeat note. Someone will be a victor. But it's hard for me to enjoy those things now. I know the truth about what we control. Nothing.

Reluctant Believer

I'm a reluctant believer. I want to trust, but verify, my relationship with God, but he defies verification. I can't fly recognizance over heaven. He offers a little evidence of his presence and love once in a while, but nothing like the presence and love I felt from Carla when we occupied the same time and space. Carla was like God with skin on. I want to trust him, but can I? Is he more trustworthy than he is dangerous, or vice versa? I think 'trustworthy' is the right answer, but my heart still aches as though a bowling ball dropped on my chest.

If I could see my situation from God's perspective, I wonder what I might observe. Would it look like God's power is limited? Would He be grieving in frustration that I can't discern between a good God and a dangerous one? Would He be angry with Satan (again) for dishing out lies that look like truth to me? Would He be proud of me for facing tough questions head on, or would He want to grab me by the collar and say, as He did to Job, "Now you listen up…?"

A Bandaid God

Do we only believe in a Bandaid God—a God who kisses us and makes it all better when we hurt? Or do we love a dangerous God—one who seems capricious and arbitrary, but who has a plan that he keeps secret from us? That's his trump card. He can always say, "I can explain it again, but you still won't understand because these things are too wonderful for you to know." He's the maker and the taker.

Maybe clergy (and other Christians) need to give pain at least equal time. If we cast God as Santa Claus, a perpetual good guy, we're missing a major part of what he would have us know about life and about him. He's the Man of Sorrows, acquainted with grief. That hour of prayer when he sweat blood was 59 minutes of anguish followed by one moment of peace, but we only hear the peace in the profound statement, "Thy will be done." Job got more kids and more wealth than he had before, but he still lived 140 years with sadness in his face, grieving what he lost. If we focus on the good stuff without recognizing the hard, bitter truth about its context, we deceive ourselves and mislead those around us. Grace only makes sense when it comes from a context of pain—real, bitter, inconsolable pain; the pain of a broken world—*my* broken world.

When was the last time you shed a tear for the misery of life—your own or someone else's? When was the last time you felt the chill that every homeless person knows intimately, or the hunger of a child who has only eaten one meal in the last two days, and that was a bit of tasteless rice? When was the last time you sensed the fear of billions who live in superstition of a deity that has no mercy?

Now, when do you think the Man of Sorrows last felt the weight of the misery of life that we take for granted? Does he feel it now and always? If he somehow incorporates pain and grace in every moment, can we learn to do it too?

Grief as Worship

Cathedrals in Europe took centuries to build. I marvel at the vision the architects must have had, fully aware they would not see the fruits of their labors in their lifetimes. I feel as though I am the architect of my grief, but I must be contented to dream of its end for I will never see it as long as I breathe. But will it be a thing of beauty? Only God knows…

Can grief be a thing of worship, like a cathedral? When Job got the news about his family, he tore his robe, shaved his head, and worshipped. If grief can be worship, what might it include? Is there room for self-pity, for fear and anger and hurt? Or is there only room for lyric poetry, for "The Lord gives and the Lord takes away. Blessed be the name of the Lord," for "Not my will be done, but yours" and other pleasant conclusions. Does agony have anything to do with worship? Grief is certainly work, and work can be worship, so is grief worship according to an algebraic formula?

Worship helps me find my place with God. Grief does that better than praise does. Grief strips us of the unessential and leaves an authenticity unrivaled by celebration without lament. So let the lamentations resume so I can see God and know my place with him.

Holy Grief

The tunnel of grief is a holy place,
A cavern of wisdom and care;
A setting to meet God face to face
And share every shred of despair.

Priorities change from the burden of grief,
We shed our familiar facade.
Our souls, in search of pain's relief,
Discover a hunger for God.

With eyes dimmed by tears we catch a view
Of life as it's meant to be.
A sorrowing soul can be renewed
And sadness can set it free.

So look for revival that only flows
From rivers of sorrow and pain.
And reach for the Lord as one who knows
The holiness grief can attain.

Old Love, New Beetle

Twenty-five years ago this month, Marybeth and I started dating in my little red bug. We loved that car and drove if for twelve years. It was stolen and recovered twice, and we had several offers to sell it before we were ready. We finally sold it in California because we knew the heater couldn't handle Michigan weather, but Bugs have held a spot in our hearts ever since. When the New Beetles started coming out, Marybeth took notice. She admired the ad that said, "The New Beetle. All new features. Like heat." She dropped hints that she preferred bright blue and a stick shift.

Tonight, after supper at her brother's family, Jim suggested we go to the barn to see something really cool. We walked out to find a blue New Beetle with a big red ribbon on top and a rosebud in the bud vase. The poem on the window went like this:

My Best Friend

> You're my best friend for twenty-five years
> Through joy and laughter, sorrow and tears,
> I sensed your heart begin to tug
> When you fell in love with my little red Bug.
>
> As through the years our love has grown
> I know you hoped for one of your own.
> You dropped some hints you wanted blue,
> So here it is. This Bug's for you.
>
> Love,
> Ken

It's the symbolism. It's a connection with our history. It's a reflection of our love. It's a wonderful surprise in a year of deepest sorrow. It's what Carla would have wanted for her mom. It has the power to help us heal. Although I've lost plenty of sleep to anguish this year, the last two weeks I've lost sleep for joy. I'd wake up in the middle of the night and smile from ear to ear with the pleasure of knowing the surprise. And now, it's Marybeth's turn to beam for joy.

Not Afraid to Live

If I Must Live

If I must live, then let me be
A mirror of your light,
To burn men's shackles, set them free,
To give the blind their sight.

If I must live, then show me how
To eat from heaven's hand.
Entrust your wisdom to endow
What I misunderstand.

If I must live, then guide my thoughts
In paths of righteousness,
Forgiving though forgetting not
My sins still un-confessed.

If I must live, then let me feel
The strength of heaven's bonds
And be my compass, be my keel
Through storms that lie beyond.

If I must live, then bind my heart
Much closer to your own,
And when I die, make me a part
Of those around your throne.

Meaning

I am wrestling with the most basic of questions such as, What is the meaning of life? So far, I think we aren't given the option of seeing meaning in any manner that is even close to the way God sees it. We see things in sequence, time and space. God sees things, people, and events without those boundaries. We view eternity as time without end, but I think God sees eternity as time without end or beginning.

This morning, a few answers came. Last night as I looked at the stars, it struck me that I should not be looking for THE meaning of life, but rather the MEANINGS of life—plural. Then this morning I thought of this answer: **The purpose of life is to be mystified, to be awestruck, to be satisfied with not understanding the ways of God.** We ought to be equally mystified by the seeming randomness of pain as by the beauty of nature. We can be nothing but awed by the vastness of the universe, by not knowing if life exists elsewhere, by the changing of the seasons, by the magnificent way we are made, by the depth of our pain when heartache comes, by love, by…

If these are our purposes, then learning is their fulfillment. We can be driven to learn of our world and our place in it, to probe deeper into the mysteries, but always knowing that we cannot know all. We can study with the assurance that our study will be eternal. Most of our study, perhaps 99% is of looking backward - learning what others have learned and recorded in history, literature, arts and sciences. But the frontier of faith is that remaining 1% where we probe the unknown, where we explore new territory, but always with the understanding that there is no limit to what we can discover. Perhaps this is joy.

If joy is understanding that we will never understand all, then I can see how current American living standards have damaged joy. Our history has been to use our wealth and knowledge to demystify life. We have advanced the boundaries of technology to explore the universe and the human body and mind. Are we at risk of being contented with what we know, and thereby depriving ourselves of the joy of curiosity?

The qualifications I want to put on accepting God's mystery are shaped by grief. It is easier to be mystified by tragedy that happens to others - the Holocaust, the Oklahoma City bombing, natural disasters, even traffic deaths, cancer, and disability that touches others we know. But when grief is personal, and when I understand that more grief can come to me just as randomly as did this first grief, I am gripped with terror more than mystery. Fear drives out joy. I'd rather demystify God than worship him when I'm aggrieved.

The purpose of man is to be mystified by, rather than to demystify, the person of God. Mystery has built-in obsolescence. When one part of the mystery seems to be solved, another presents itself. The challenge is to learn to live with perpetual mystery. Can I be OK with a God that only reveals himself partially? Can I be OK when the part I see and know through grief is not pain-free? When I can affirm that kind of God, I think I'll be OK again.

Curiosity

This morning I discovered something wonderful and profound. We saw a ladybug at the window as we were eating breakfast. Marybeth observed it closely and described a detail of its design to Dan. I found myself struck that God designed such intricate details into his creation. I asked why, and the answer that came back was, "God wants me to be forever curious about him. He wants us to keep looking for him in creation and in the way he works in our lives. Our natural curiosity is God-hunger."

We can be curious about many things, and perhaps some are more meaningful than others. Curiosity about illicit enterprises is less meaningful than curiosity about science or art. The more honorable pursuits are those that reach for eternity - for God himself. I have this image of us straining, persisting, sometimes grasping for truth, always hungry for more, and always knowing that our discoveries will not be the last. There will always be deeper truths, higher purposes to strive for. There will always be new frontiers that require strides of logic, leaps of faith and a willingness to abandon current knowledge in order to embrace new knowledge.

When it comes to matters of God, I think we need to abandon understanding in order to understand him. We need to accept that our understanding will be limited until we get to heaven. Period. End of discussion. That does not imply that we should abandon our pursuit of God. On the contrary, we should pursue him all the more for he is the author of truth. But we should view God as the holder of all new surprises, the writer of wisdom, the inventor of invention, the founder of frontiers. Some might view his unfathomable character as a barrier. "If we cannot understand him, then why try?" they might say. But I say true joy comes in pursuing him knowing that as soon as we are delighted by one discovery, another is planned for us.

Faith in Me

I understand so little of
How faith in God begins,
Or why he chooses me to gain
His payment for my sins.
But I give praise for saving faith
With all its mystery;
It's not for works that I have done,
For he plants faith in me.

But when I disobediently
Exert my right of choice,
He waits until the moment
I am ready for his voice.
He patiently restores my soul
And calls me back to see,
Although my faith in him may fail,
He still has faith in me.

And when my days have reached their end
And I am called above
To face the master of our lives
With flawed, imperfect love,
My joy will be complete as he
Reviews my history.
"The slate is clean, come in my friend,
For you had faith in me."

Traditions

I have no regrets about my relationship with Carla, and for that I am deeply grateful. I am not a perfect Dad, but I believe I have struck a good balance, and I have no regrets. I am grateful for so many roles that I played in Carla's life. At the top of my list is our "nights out." We started this tradition, at Marybeth's suggestion, about six or seven years ago. I try to take out each of the kids once a month. Carla had the first Wednesday, Jill the second, Dan the third, and then Marybeth and I would have a date the fourth week. We weren't completely consistent, especially as I traveled more or when we were on vacation, but we didn't miss too many months. Carla still enjoyed them, even as she became more independent, and so did I. We'd pick a restaurant that she wanted most of the time, and we'd talk about anything and everything. We'd usually go shopping afterwards, but not necessarily to buy anything unless there was a family birthday coming up, or Christmas. Sometimes we'd do something else like go for a walk, rent a movie, or practice driving the car at a church parking lot when she was a student driver. The main thing was that we were together. What a great tradition!

We have also had great vacations. Some of the best consisted of just renting a cottage and lounging around, but we also saw great areas of the country like Colorado, California, Florida, Maine and lots of places in between. I'm sure I complained about the cost sometimes, but I'm so glad we did them. Marybeth has been a wonderful engineer of other family traditions. Decorated birthday cakes have been one of her trademarks. Christmas traditions include cutting our own tree Thanksgiving weekend and decorating it together, making spritz cookies and gingerbread houses. I always viewed these traditions as a time to build memories that we could enjoy the rest of our lives. Little did I realize just how precious they would be.

But new traditions are also taking their place beside the old ones. A dog-wood tree blooms in the back yard around Carla's birthday. It was a gift from friends at church, and is lighted every night with strings of white and purple Christmas lights. We bring flowers to the cemetery on special days and take time off to commemorate her birthday as though it is a holiday. New traditions add enrichment in their own way.

God's Language

I wonder if God's language is the language of feelings rather than the language of our intellect. Our most common communication is inadequate to describe the most important things of life. Words help us give shape to our musings, but feelings let us go beyond words to explore the deepest mysteries of life. Feelings and intuition pick up where intellect and words end. Maybe that is why God tells us to be still and know that he is God. That's when our comprehension can take another dimension, but not before we are disciplined enough to be quiet. Interestingly, our words give us some ability to control ourselves and others. Perhaps that's another reason God tells us to be quiet. He wants us to relinquish control.

Trust and Obey

Yesterday, Marybeth and I both woke up with a simultaneous conclusion about how to make this experience an experience of grace. Trust and obey. That's the bottom line. We have to trust God for answers to unanswerable questions, knowing we won't get them in this life. We have to trust that he knows what he's doing to enrich us now. Our job is to obey him by watching what he's doing and joining him in his work. That may mean writing and speaking for me. For Marybeth, it may mean painting and mothering. Maybe it will mean other things as well, but our job is to watch for them. There seem to be a million ways to remind me of my grief and only a handful to relieve it. And sometimes not even one of the handful works. But trust and obey seems to be the final answer. Easier said than done.

Psalm 23

I've seen something in Psalm 23 that I never saw before. The first three verses talk about God in the third person.

> The Lord is my shepherd, I shall not be in want.

> **He** makes me lie down in green pastures,

> **He** leads me beside quiet waters,

> **He** restores my soul.

> **He** guides me in paths of righteousness for his name's sake.

Then in verse four, something happens. The pronoun changes from **he** to **you**.

> Even though I walk through the valley of the shadow of death,

> I will fear no evil, for **you** are with me;

> **Your** rod and **your** staff, they comfort me.

> **You** prepare a table before me in the presence of my enemies.

> **You** anoint my head with oil; my cup overflows.

> Surely goodness and love will follow me all the days of my life,

> And I will dwell in the house of the Lord forever.

What changes the Psalmist's perspective in verse four? A walk through the valley of the shadow of death changes more than his perspective. That makes the relationship personal. That's my story too. God is in my face with this experience, and now it's personal. I can't talk about him in the third person anymore. He has engaged me, and I must engage him. My loss is real, and God had something to do with it. I spoke about God before as though he was an object. Life was easier then. I could pretend to put him away when I was done with him. But death changes everything. Now I need him like never before, and I want his comfort. I can't just talk **about** him. I have to talk **to** him. The rest of the Psalm doesn't provide answers to the hardest questions. It just provides God, and it paints him in word pictures as a personal, gracious, caring Shepherd for a needy lamb like me.

Made of Clay

I am a terra cotta bowl,
For common use each day.
Though some may think me quite ornate,
I'm only made of clay.

For value isn't measured by
My sturdiness or pride,
But rather by the love I share
From treasures found inside.

And even riches I may hold,
And wisdom, I believe,
Are gifts of God who freely lends
To those who would receive.

So I am but a fragile pot,
A humble lump of clay
To be filled up and then poured out,
And soon to fade away.

But all's not lost, for though I pass,
The goodness that I share
Lives on in those who catch these grains,
The souls for whom I care.

Time to Grieve

I may be back to my routines,
A thousand ritualistic means
To earn my way and fill the day
With memos, meetings, calls and more;
But don't mistake such things as these
As what I might be living for.

The only loss you may detect
Is loss of innocence. In fact,
You probably can't sense anything's
Amiss as I pursue a dozen goals,
Amass a legend, make my mark,
Fulfill a score of hollow roles.

But in my heart of hearts there lies
A yearning I won't compromise.
It's pointless to inspire me
With tales of what I might achieve
My hopes and dreams are tempered now,
For I have taken time to grieve.

Those aspirations have their place—
They benefit the human race.
But don't confuse their value with
The blessings kept for those who grieve.
For loss can strip agendas clean,
And make you own what you believe.

The Cross by the Side of the Road

My memories often bring comfort and joy,
Though some can bring heartache instead.
I smile to think how she acted so coy
And chuckle at things that she said.

Whenever I visit her bedroom I hear
The laughter that used to be there.
A glance at her brush usually brings out a tear,
Remembering the feel of her hair.

I seldom approach the town or the school
Without a new thought of my loss.
For she was my hope, my delight and my jewel,
But now all that's left is a cross.

The accident site is right on the way
To everywhere we have to go.
Her friends brought a wreath and a symbol to say
What most of us already know.

This is the place where her soul was set free
And ours gained a burdensome load.
Remember sweet Carla whenever you see
The cross by the side of the road.

Hope's Half-life

When disappointments overwhelm,
When safety disappears,
Despair can plant its heartless seeds,
Confirm our darkest fears.

When hope is suddenly cut in half
And then in half again,
You may be shocked to find that Hope's
Half-life can never end.

Balance of Power

I've also been thinking about the balance of power between God and Satan. We think of God as being all-powerful, and I believe he is in the end. But we're not at the end. We're in the middle, and in the middle there is this incredible struggle going on. I saw a T-shirt that says it best. On the front it said, "Jesus Saves." On the back it said, "Satan Sucks." They are both part of the same T-shirt. Sure Jesus saves, but we only need a savior because Satan sucks.

The devil is hard at it. He's messing with us all the time. Carla's death was not because of a specific sin, but it was because sin is in everything, everywhere, in such a non-specific manner. I think we're more tainted than we know—more stained and dirty by the filth around and in us. We get used to it and think it is somehow normal, but it's not. It's not supposed to be here. And death is a part of that. It's not supposed to be here either. But it is because Satan is. Satan Sucks! Death Be Damned!

I guess I'm surprised at how powerful Satan is, and how weak God seems to be. He's got the ultimate victory, I'm sure, but we have to slug it out between now and eternity. I took so much for granted. So many people believe at such a shallow level. "God said it. I believe it. That's that." They probably have no clue just how sin permeates us and our world, just as I was limited in my understanding. They probably have no concept of how much cleanup God has to do.

So how can I summarize the lesson *du jour?* I have a deeper appreciation for God because I have a deeper appreciation for his enemy—for my enemy. I'm shocked that I haven't hated Satan like he deserves. I'm equally shocked that I took God for granted to such a degree. I think I can even find it in my heart to say "Thank you" to God for providing a way of escape from this filthy life. We think we've got it so good, but still we're desperate for a shower, the kind that cleans our souls.

Two Feet

My feet are planted, true to form,
In not one place, but two.
And as I shift my weight, I find
It shapes my point of view.

While one boot sloshes through the mud
The other walks on air.
For earth retains the leather sole,
But heaven claims its pair.

Joy

Joy is gradually being redefined, like safety and providence and so many other concepts. I have always thought of it as happiness, like a babbling brook. Now I understand it is more like a serious river, like the Missouri, the Nile, or the Danube. It is deep and wide. It flows steadily, even over major boulders or waterlogged oaks, without so much as a ripple. It provides routes for exploration of new territories, like Lewis and Clark used the Missouri to open the West. It offers a home, not for diminutive, sunny, rainbow trout, but for the likes of sturgeon and other giants of the waterways. It makes buoyancy possible for commercial barges and paddle-wheelers, pleasure boats and tugs. It links people together across cultural boundaries and time, across belief systems and races. It gathers strength from a thousand babbling brooks with a nod of thanks to each one, then delivers the freshness of their waters to a thousand thirsty farms and fields.

The Joy of Job

When we think of the virtues of Job, the first thing that usually comes to mind is his patience. I'm not sure where that label comes from. I don't see it in the book. In fact, I see a pretty impatient, angry and confused subject. He didn't take his suffering sitting down. He was a first class whiner. He challenged God to a trial by jury. He crowed about his righteousness. He was spittin' bullets. He probably couldn't verbalize everything he felt, but it's pretty clear that he was anything but patient.

So why do we think of him as patient? Maybe its because we can't imagine ourselves having to endure such injustice, such pain. Anyone who doesn't kill himself under such circumstances must be patient, we assert, resigning ourselves to a different fate. Patience must be the only thing that kept him from suicide.

Maybe we also like to think that if we just wait out difficulties, we'll get our due like Job did. Because he was patient, we reason, he got twice as much as what he had before. If he wasn't patient, he would have been a loser. The moral of the story seems to be that you get more stuff by being patient with God. If you can take what he shovels out, grin and bear it, then God will reward you. Just be patient.

Do you think he knew how the story would end? Not on your life.

I don't think the Book of Job is about patience at all. In fact, the book isn't about Job. He seems like the main character, but he's not. I don't think there's anything special about Job. He sounds like he could be anybody. OK, maybe he was righteous, but so are a lot of people. He could have been like the guy next door. He could have been like you.

The Book of Job offers a rare glimpse of who God is, without the "spin doctors" around to cast him in a Santa Claus role. God speaks with his own voice - not once, but twice. And he offers solid speeches both times. These weren't just brief one-liners. They were in-your-face heart-to-heart talks between God and this guy who could be anybody. If this is a story of patience, I'd say it is about God's patience.

God holds his tongue through all Job's whining and crying. He holds his tongue while each of the so-called friends tries to speak for God. He watches the drama unfold and somehow manages to control his temper enough to not call Job to task for shaking his fist at the Creator. The Almighty didn't have to put up with Job's self-righteous whimpering and pitiful sobbing. All he had to do was nod and the Enemy would have finished him off. But God was patient with Job—this nobody—this anybody.

If Job displayed any virtue at all, it didn't really come until the closing chapters, and especially the closing verses of the book. The unlikely virtue was joy, but probably not the kind most people would recognize. First, Job apologizes to God. Can you imagine, this pawn in a chess game of the highest dimension apologizing to the one who consciously allowed—even ordained—his pain? But he does. And then he follows it with a statement even more profound. Job says, "I was speaking of things too wonderful for me to know." Now that's joy!

This joy probably was expressed with a long face, a tired face, a face that showed battle-weariness in the extreme. It probably lacked a smile. It probably was not a light-hearted face. I picture sadness in this joy. I picture deep-set eyes that have no twinkle. But I also picture a quiet assurance—born of terror that has matured into peace. It's a peace that defies explanation, but it is unmistakable nonetheless. And because this peace exists without cause—in spite of horrendous circumstances—there is joy.

Balance

My wrestling was met with Isaiah 43:1 yesterday. "Fear not, for I have redeemed you." I recognized that my anger at God was basically fear—of an unsafe God. Then I noticed that God's answer to fear isn't a promise of safety but rather a promise of redemption. It is as though redemption overwhelms human issues, like safety, so much that safety doesn't deserve a reference in a headline. It's like saying, "I know you're thirsty, but it's Christmas." At first they don't seem to have anything to do with each other, but on second thought, they have everything to do with each other.

I took it a bit further. I think most of us view ourselves as equal parts human and spirit, like a one-to-one ratio. And it's no surprise. Humanity is our only tangible reference point. We begin to grasp an awareness of our spirit from recognizing that our humanity doesn't have all the answers. But perhaps this verse gives us a clue as to the true ratio between the soul and the body. Maybe it is something like ten-to-one, a hundred-to-one, or even a thousand-to-one, or more... The spiritual truth so outweighs our human comprehension that Job can only apologize to God for speaking of things too wonderful for him to know.

This seems to be collaborated in other parts of the Bible as well. When a crippled man is lowered before Christ from the roof, Christ forgives his sins before he heals him. Matthew talks about seeking the kingdom of God first, and all these things (human needs) will be met as well. Jesus didn't concern himself with tangible needs, and although he died a pauper (in human terms), his ministry was humanity's greatest inheritance. The Lord's Prayer devotes one phrase to human issues—"give us this day our daily bread"—but the rest of it focuses on spiritual issues.

This perspective seems to devalue our humanness, but somehow I can live with it. I find comfort in seeing my human pain completely overwhelmed by God's redemption. This must be what soul-weaning is all about. **We are not so much humans on a spiritual journey as we are spirits on a human journey.**

A Thousand To One

My body and soul were intertwined
In equal portions, it seemed;
When one was weak, the other was strong,
Except when they double-teamed.

But tragedy struck my humanness
And ripped my soul to shreds.
A logical faith was soon displaced
By thousands of pieces instead.

And as the mosaic rearranged
Itself at the Master's hand,
A picture emerged I wouldn't have guessed,
Though now I understand.

Our humanness is *one small piece*
When all is said and done;
But spiritual peace outshines the rest
At least a thousand-to-one.

Awesome and Awful

I am struck by the similarity between the words "awful" and "awesome." They are so close together, yet so far apart. This is mystery, but I think there is a clue to God's identity in this. To fear him is to begin to be wise. Job talks about God being "too wonderful." I sense that I may be on the verge of discovery of the awesomeness that follows awfulness. I'm ready.

I have also reflected on how the will of God may work with our will. It is like the brain and the hand. The brain senses an itch and sends an invitation to the hand to scratch it. The hand is directed by the brain, but it can refuse to cooperate. If you don't believe the hand is free to choose, just ask a quadriplegic. He can muster all his will, but the hand still refuses. When the hand and the brain are working in tandem, the itch gets scratched in an apparently effortless way. I think that is how God's and man's will work. God is the brain, and man is the hand.

International Service

Less than a year after Carla's death, I was invited to explore a new avenue of service. I received a call from a former client, a physician in Appalachia, to join him in establishing a Christian medical group practice in Romania. The invitation came as my father was dying of cancer (he died just before Christmas, the same year as Carla), but it did not take me long to recognize the value that two weeks involved in ministry in another culture might do for me. The lessons turned out to be even more profound than I anticipated.

I was changed forever by the experience. I found it to be a perfect fit for my skills and interests, combining business and ministry to demonstrate the value of ethical dealings, serving as a model of employment in an emerging market economy, and showing how God works to transform lives. Healthcare is a universal vehicle for showing the love of God in every culture, and this clinic is at the apex of that kind of ministry for masses of people with hungry souls. God is doing a beautiful thing, both for Romania and for me.

Since the first visit, I have extended myself into further international service. Romania has given me a standing invitation, which I intend to accept annually, and I've also been drawn to serve as a healthcare management consultant in Kyrgyzstan and Honduras, with an eye to other needs as they become apparent. I think I have never felt so completely and consistently in the will of God as I have through these experiences. My skills are a perfect fit for the needs, and the warm and intimate relationships that developed so quickly enabled me to accomplish more than I expected. When I'm serving in these ways, I feel as though the hosts of heaven surround me for encouragement, concentration, understanding and energy. Carla is with me, joined by many others who are cheering me on. I am finding joy again. I am finding it in sharing of myself, fully and without reservation. I am finding joy in catching a vision of what God is up to, and of how I can participate in it.

The needs are compelling. They speak to the core of my soul and draw out the best in me. I sense God's leading as He provides both the opportunities and the means for service, with the love and support of my family and friends.

Too Wonderful for Me

Inspired by Psalms 131 and 139, and Job 42

Lord, give me simple, childlike faith,
A faith that need not see
Nor hear, nor touch, nor taste of things
Too wonderful for me.

Lord, calm my soul with gentle strokes
Of queenly sovereignty.
And wean my heart with hope of things
Too wonderful for me.

I rest myself in your embrace,
I bow on bended knee.
For you're the author of all things
Too wonderful for me.

Treasures

Sadness is so pervasive. There is no corner of my imagination or psyche that is untouched by it. Anything and everything can make me shudder with grief—a memory, an artifact from the Carla era or even something that reminds me of an artifact, a hope I once had that suddenly comes to mind, but can no longer come true. No wonder grief is disabling. How can it be otherwise? If it were not disabling, it would be forgotten, but it cannot be forgotten. The pain of forgetting is far greater than the pain of remembering. This loss is a fact of history—my personal history. No amount of time will erase that. No amount of faith will alter what has happened. All that remains to be changed is the symbolism associated with the history—the enduring lessons of life. Contrary to the persistent adage, time does not heal. Time only helps us learn to live with pain.

What timeless lessons, what treasures of darkness, have I learned so far?

I've learned that we don't own ourselves, but that God somehow gives order to life much more mysteriously than we can ever comprehend. I've learned that there are no accidents, but that God uses horrible disasters to bring about his perfect will. I don't know if he causes them or allows them, but I can live with that mystery—partly because I have no other choice, and partly because I would choose to if I did have a choice. I choose to believe that God is ultimately good, despite the pain I endure at his hand, because I have seen at least as much evidence of his holiness and majesty as I have seen of his destructive power. And I long for his holiness more than I fear his power.

I've learned that salvation is worth more than any loss. God wants us to have a restored relationship with him so much that he sacrificed his son, risked him for eternity, to make sure we could be reunited with our Creator and other Christians for eternity. God's answer to our deepest fears is his plan of redemption, of reconnecting with him. In essence, he is saying that death isn't worth fearing nearly as much as separation from him. He's saying that the fear and the pain of losing someone we love is far outweighed by the gift of eternal life.

There is pain in every life, and every person must face their pain if it is to teach them timeless truths. Fear compels us to avoid pain at all costs, to defer it or deflect it, but to do anything but face it head on is to postpone the inner peace that we long for. Confronting pain is terrifying, because it ultimately brings us face to face with our own mortality. We have to come to grips with the fact that we all will die, and that readiness is better than disbelief or ignorance. And that brings us full circle to the first treasure of darkness—that we don't belong to ourselves and that readiness for our own mortality somehow requires us to decide what we're going to do about God. We can choose to hate him, fear him, avoid, or ignore him, but we do so at the risk of missing his holiness, his mystery, and his plan to restore us to himself. And missing all that is far more tragic than the consequence of any other alternative.

So there you have it, one person's perspective on the purposes of life—insights gained from a very grueling and truth-rending path. Ponder these treasures of darkness. Let them simmer in the corners of your mind and the crevices of your heart. Ignore them if you dare, and savor them if you will. If your heart is broken, I urge you to run for help. You'll find it in the Bible, in the loving arms of Christian friends and counselors, and in the quietness of a personal relationship with your Creator.

Treasures of Darkness
Inspired by Isaiah 45

Lord of the Evening, Lord of the Light,
Lord of the strong and the lame,
Fill me with wonder, capture my soul,
Lord of all, know me by name.

Teach me of sorrow, teach me of pain,
Teach me of grief and of grace.
Treasures of darkness, riches abound
Stored in your secret place.

King of disaster, King of repose,
King of the lion and lamb,
Level the mountains, cut through the bars,
Leave me no doubt whose I am.

Praise the Creator, praise to the Lord,
Praise him for making us whole.
There is no other god beside you;
Thank you for saving my soul.

Your Servant Today

Lord, I have preferred my own way.
My nature is not to obey.
When I'm in control
My compromised soul
Cannot find your peace, come what may.

Let perfect submission portray
The spirit of Christ as he lay
His life for your soul.
He gave up control
So you may find peace day by day.

As babes in their mother's arms lay
Bring comfort to me Lord, I pray.
For life to be full,
I'll give up control.
Take me as your servant today.

Ballast in the Bow

I saw myself as captain
Of a gleaming luxury
Filled up with valued treasures
And bound for destiny.

I left the harbor proudly
And set my sights abroad
With confidence and safety,
With skills and faith in God.

My course was undetermined
Except in broadest terms.
Into the wind I headed
With speed and rudder firm.

The trip was uneventful
And pleasant on the way.
Adventure would escape me
Until that tragic day.

The storm hit me like lightning
Without a notice fair.
The ship was rocked with thunder
But God seemed not to care.

My sails were ripped to pieces
The mast stood tall no more.
The wind and rain tore through me
And chilled me to the core.

I faced my God with terror
And begged for his relief.
My treasures lost their value;
I sank into the reef.

"I'm sorry for your pain," he said.
His tears rolled down my cheeks.
He threw a lifeline to me,
Then he let me drift for weeks.

The weeks turned into months
While floating on the shelf.
As months turned into years,
My ship rebuilt itself.

This new ship handles weather
So much better than before.
It's seaworthy and stable
When I'm away from shore.

I sail again with confidence
But I'm not captain now.
I sail as crew and add my pain
To ballast in the bow.

Freedom

Loss gives freedom through its bondage. It's strange. Very strange.

The bondage of loss is undeniable. I'm reminded of the unchangeable character of my loss every time I see her picture, conjure a memory, trip over a sentiment, or am overwhelmed by a wave of grief for no apparent reason. It is painfully accentuated when I'm faced with how all things are possible with God. It strikes again when I comprehend the meaningless-ness of life, the pointless pursuit of happiness. I read it in my face when I look in a mirror, or see my reflection in the eyes of my friends. The bars of sadness are my constant companion. There is no escape but death itself.

But somehow, in the midst of this ever-present prison, I find freedoms that I never knew existed. I am free:

- to feel sad without guilt

- to follow my heart with relentless energy

- to embrace pain in others and encourage them to see it as a teacher

- to question God about everything without needing His answers

- to establish livable limits to my activities and pursuits

There is something honorable—even holy—about this confinement. I sense that I am closer to truth and beauty than I have ever been. It is as though pain is lifeblood, to me and to those who walk in it with me.

A speaker at a conference I went to recently asked his large audience how many had pagers, cell phones, email or other trappings of time-pressed professionals. Everyone raised their hands. Then he asked how many felt like they had more time because of these so-called time-savers. No one raised their hand—except me. But it didn't take long for me to realize that my sense of freedom came *in spite of technology rather than because of it.* My sense of freedom, of more time, of clear priorities, came from the prison of my loss. It came from knowing in the soul of my soul that my priorities are properly aligned, once and for all, thanks to the profound loss of my daughter.

Nothing, NOTHING, is more important than the pursuit of God. That's what Carla did, and that's all that mattered in the end. Every other pursuit pales in comparison. Every other pursuit leaves an insatiable hunger, no matter how great the accomplishments. That truth is now branded on my heart with inescapable pain that keeps me focused. I am free to forego all else in pursuit of God.

Afterword

Our loss seems to transcend time. As time goes on, sadness and acceptance continue to occupy the same space in my heart and mind. My soul is still unsettled, but growth continues to mold it to the mind of Christ as well.

I think a major part of acceptance comes from facing not just the loss of Carla, but by facing my own mortality as well. Life is our most precious possession, at least that is how we think of it. We think of it as ours to do with as we will. We think we're largely in charge of what kind of life we make for ourselves and for our families. We treasure those we love, and we are taught from the earliest impressions that life is worthy of our greatest honor and protection.

But Carla's death has taught me that life isn't what I thought it to be. Life is certainly valuable, but not in the same sense as it once was. I embrace life, but I would embrace death just as fully if it were to be in my path. And it will most certainly be in my path again. I do not fear death—mine or anyone else's. I know now that grief—even profound grief—is survivable, sanctifying and inspiring—though no less painful, and that my own death will be a blessing to me.

But I also have a new sense of the purposes of life. I am not my own. I never have been, although my confession of this truth has never been more true than it is now. I formerly took great personal responsibility for being all God wanted me to be, believing it was my job to figure it out. Now I accept each day as a gift of God, and I'm ready to let him have his way with me, day by day. I find enduring comfort in the idea that I'm not my own. It takes the pressure off, and gives me a new and more fulfilling challenge—to watch for God at work, and join him in his work.

So my journey continues. I'm still in the Mammoth Cave of Grief, and expect to remain here until I once again share the same time and place as Carla. But I'm growing familiar with this environment. My eyes have adjusted so that now I can see some of the rare gems that are only found here. These treasures of sorrow are invaluable, for they not only offer light in the darkness and hope for the hopeless, but they also lend meaning to life with all of its mystery. I hope my descriptions of them enrich you, whether you are in the cave with me or not.

If you are in the cave, for whatever reason, I'm sorry for your pain. I know its awfulness all too well. But I hope that you will let it teach you as it is teaching me, and that you may also share the treasures you discover.

If you are not in the cave, I hope you have a new understanding of those who are, and are better equipped to offer meaningful love and support to them. I hope that your wisdom grows from tasting of my pain, and that you may be better able to face your own pain as it comes, and to help others face theirs. I pray less for safety and more for wisdom—both yours and mine. Safety is mythical and temporal, but wisdom lasts forever.

Appendix

Address to Holland Christian High School Students

Carla Ruth Hekman died in a tragic car accident on Friday, January 9, 1998. Her dad presented these comments at a chapel service the following Monday morning before 1,000 students, teachers and staff.

Address to Holland Christian High School Students

January 12, 1998
Ken Hekman

We've asked a lot of "what ifs…" this week.

What if we had insisted she stay home?

What if she could have avoided a collision by a few seconds?

What if she were in a different car?

And we've experienced deep pain…

…from the sheriff's deputies at the door

…to identifying her body in the hospital emergency room

…to telling relatives and hearing their agonizing responses over the phone.

But there is one "what if" that we are so thankful we did not have to ask. We will be eternally grateful that we did not have to ask, "What if Carla had not committed her life to Christ?" We know she belonged to Jesus and that she was ready when he called her name. She had been touched by the death of another former Holland Christian student four years ago, her cousin Cheri Hekman, and had responded to God's invitation of salvation then. And she lived her commitment with a kindness and grace that I'm sure many of you know from direct and personal experience.

We've also experienced a lot of hugs these past few days. Hugs are good because when you give one, you get one back. Carla was a good hugger. Carla hugged me as she went out the door Friday night. That was the last hug with her earthly Dad. Her next hug was with her heavenly father. She'd been reaching out to him for a few years, and Friday night was her time to get close enough to hug him in person, and to feel his warm embrace.

So this week as you comfort each other with hugs, think of Jesus hugging Carla, and know that he wants to hug you too. And tonight when you get home, hug your parents, and let them hug you back. If they are surprised by your sudden affection, tell them what you learned in school today. Tell them hugs were invented as a reminder that God's arms can surround us with love that lasts forever, if we only get close enough to hug him back.

If you aren't ready for a Jesus hug, I urge you to talk to a teacher, a Christian friend or to your parents today. If Carla had waited until today, it would have been too late. She didn't even have time to cry out for forgiveness at the last moment. That's why we are so thankful she was already forgiven. But you can hear my voice. You have the gift of life for at least another day. Use

112

it to make the most important decision of all, and then you too can live like Carla did, reaching for the biggest bear hug of all.

Thank you for the love you have all shown to us as a family. Jill and Dan will need lots of your hugs in the days and months ahead. The loss of their big sister left a big hole in all of our hearts. With your help, that hole can be filled with love and with the assurance that they'll hug Carla again someday, as will all who answer Christ's invitation.

Thank you and God bless you.

Funeral Message for Carla Hekman

By Rev. Jim Boer

What do you think of, who do you think of when you hear the word, "conqueror?" Maybe your mind goes back in history to Alexander the Great—his military might and superior strategies laid rival kingdoms low. Or maybe you think more modern, maybe you think of a man like Bill Gates, whose ingenuity and business savvy have earned him billions. Maybe for you a conqueror is not some larger-than-life figure. Maybe for you the conquerors are a fellow student who landed all the big scholarships for college, or the co-worker who makes the breakthroughs and gets all the slaps on the back.

My guess is that none of us, over the lasts few tragic days, have used that word to describe Carla Hekman. But I am here this afternoon to say that by God's definition and in God's eyes, that is precisely what she is. As far as God is concerned, a conqueror is not someone who attains some great feat of personal achievement. As far as God is concerned, a conqueror is not the one with the biggest kingdom, the biggest bank account, or the best reputation. **No, a conqueror is one who lives in His love and in the love of His Son.**

(Romans 8:31-39)

For just a few minutes this afternoon I want you to focus your attention on three things about the love of God.

God proves the depth of his love by sending Jesus (Romans 8:32)

There is not one single person here today that wants to be here. Carla's family doesn't want to be here. Her classmates and teachers don't want to be here. I don't want to be here. Given the choice, we would go back. Given the opportunity, we would change it all. But we had no choice.

What makes the love of God so profound, so amazing, so divine, is that when it came to the death of his Son, he had a choice. He could have held back. He could have held on. Why, Jesus even begged him to reconsider. "Father, take this cup from me." But he didn't. **The Father did not spare his Son, because he could not spare us; he could not spare Carla.**

God shows the surprising heights of his love by justifying sinners. (Romans 8:33, 34)

Justification is the word the Church uses to describe that act of God in which he takes sinners, in all their guilt and shame, in all their brokenness and alienation, and makes them right. Justification is the word that describes God's total acceptance of wayward people.

One of the things that got Jesus into so much trouble was the way he would justify sinners. There was Zacchaeus, that little sawed-off swindler who deserved only to be strung up by his heals. But Jesus justified him. Then there was that woman who was caught in the act, guilty of adultery. He, who had the authority to condemn, instead scattered her accusers and sent her away forgiven. And then there was that thief on the cross—a man who had but hours, maybe minutes, to live—and Jesus, even as he died, welcomed him into eternal paradise.

Carla, a few years ago, moved deep in her soul by her cousin, Cheri's death, stood up and confessed that she too had accepted Christ's gracious invitation to be justified by his love, washed in his blood. Carla died Friday night, but she died justified.

God demonstrates the strength of his love by keeping us in the grip of his grace
(Romans 8:35, 38, 39)

What Paul is talking about in these verses are the things that act like wedges between God and his people. These are the things that threaten to come in between God and us. We feel them, don't we? We feel the strain that trouble, hardship, persecution, famine, nakedness, danger and sorrow puts on our faith. The confidence Paul wants us to have is that none of these things, no matter how they feel, can break the tie that binds. Though we are threatened on every side and at every turn, the conquering love of God in Christ keeps us in the grip of grace. Inseparable, Paul says. He lets nothing break the bond.

Death—though it has separated us from Carla, death has not separated God from Carla.

And so this is our comfort: Carla Hekman, more than a conqueror through Christ who loved her.

I have to ask you, is Christ's conquering love alive in you as it was alive in Carla? Are you pursuing your victory based on personal achievement or are you living in the victory of Christ's love. If ever there was a time to ponder your salvation, to examine your standing, now is the time. For all the facades have been torn away. There is no place to run to, nowhere to hide. The reality of our human vulnerability and finitude is naked before us. Will you accept the invitation Jesus offers you today, the invitation to live in his love? If you're hesitating, let me remind you of what Jesus said. "What good is it for a man to gain the whole world, yet lose his soul?"

Come to the Savior now.

Before I conclude I want to say a few words to this family.

Ken,   My friend, your faith has sustained you, but your witness has
         changed us.

Marybeth,   What we want for you we cannot have. You have lost
              both a daughter and a friend. Our prayer for you is
              unfading memories.

Jill and Dan,   Your parents love you so much. You two are so special. You
                  have carried so much these last few days. We all want you
                  to know that our hearts, our ears and our arms will always
                  be open to you.

Classmates, teachers and friends,   Your loud tears have not only been
                                      a fitting tribute but a genuine
                                      comfort to this family. Thank you
                                      for your love, your prayers, your
                                      hugs and your faith.

Excerpts from Carla Hekman's prayer journal

A few weeks after her death, we found a journal Carla kept by her bedside, containing over 90 prayers she wrote in the past several months. It has been a source of inspiration and incredible comfort to us, so we'd like to share excerpts with you.

Please, dear Jesus, enter my life and help me to make *you* the focus.

Thank you for blessing me with so many worldly possessions, friends, a great family, and love. You are such a mighty, powerful God, and I am blown away by your strength and depth.

You are an awesome and holy God. Thank you for letting me be a Christian.

You are such an awesome God. My favorite part of your creation is the clouds. They show your majesty and glory at its finest.

You are my only comfort in life and in death, so I'm sure you can help me through these turbulent teenage years.

Thank you for my teachers. Thank you for my other friends. Thank you for my family. Help me to show them how much I appreciate them.

Please be with the royal family in England as they mourn Diana's death.

God, you are an awesome God, a God of power and mercy, a God who rules over the earth with majesty. I am totally in awe of you. Thank you for bringing me a little closer to you. Please help me continue wanting to be like Jesus, and guide me in my journey.

Please forgive me for being selfish, help me be a more caring person. Make me a servant. Also Lord, please be with the boys who were in the accident this morning, and be with all their friends as they grieve and pray. *Thank you* for blessing HCHS. We've been so fortunate, thus far.

Thank you for church and thank you for Mom and Dad. Please be with Dad as he travels and works - keep him safe.

Help me to focus only on the important things in life (with you in the center, of course) and not be distracted by minor details. However, don't let me miss out on the simple joys in life either. I love you Lord.

You are an awesome God! I am so amazed at your glory and power and mercy. You are all-knowing and all-caring. Thank you for being the Lord of my life. Help me to always remember who I am and especially *whose* I am.

Thank you for dying on the cross to save me from my sins. Please help me to see myself as you see me: a wonderful person with lots of potential. Please help me to use the gifts you've given me to my full ability and help me choose a future that pleases you and goes according to your wonderful and perfect plan for my life. Please help me see what it is you want me to do with my life—what you want me to be.

Thank you for this day. Help me remember not to take life for granted. All the great times I remember having as a child are now gone—lost forever. Please don't let me let life just slip away, often unnoticed. Let me always be aware of how great the routine parts of life are.

God you are so wonderful. Thank you for showing yourself to me through nature.

I know that sometimes I make too big a deal about little things. Please help me keep things in perspective.

Thank you for always listening to my prayers. You are an awesome God. You are majestic and wonderful and all-powerful. I love you Lord and I want you to be the King of my life.

Thank you for the teachers and the hard work they put into each day's lesson, and their dedication to Jesus and to teaching. Let them never forget their ultimate goal.

I can't wait to get to college, Lord. Even more, I can't wait to face the "real world." I can't wait to have a real job, a husband, dogs, kids, a home. Please help me to slow down and enjoy every second of my life as it is right now.

Thank you that I have such a good relationship with my parents. Also, thanks that Jill and I and Dan and I get along so well most of the time.

Thank you for keeping me safe in the horrible weather tonight. Thank you for the snow. It's so beautiful, Lord. I love it! You are so powerful. You are the master of beauty. I can see the beauty of your face reflected in your awesome creation, oh God. Please keep me safe as driving will be hazardous now.

Thank you for being a friend to me as well as a teacher, a Savior and my God. I know I'm at a difficult point in my life and everything really confuses me right now, but I have nothing to fear because you are my walking buddy on the road of life. And if it gets too hard for me to go on alone, you will be there to carry me through it. Thank you Lord!

Thank you for watching over me today. Thank you for keeping me safe. Lord, I really feel like you have something important planned for me. Please help me to figure out what you have in mind and please grant me the wisdom and strength and the courage to carry it out. I know my life is not just an accident, the things that have happened to me and to those around me are not just coincidental. Please help me piece everything together to find out what I should do for others.

Please be with all my friends and remind them of your presence. Help me to be a blessing to them and to everyone else around me.

Thank you for keeping me safe on the road so far; please continue to keep me safe as winter approaches.

Thank you for my wonderful family. Thank you for making me feel special. Thank you for close relationships with family members. Thank you for Pooh.

Please keep everyone I know (and others too!) safe as the roads will get slick soon.

Thank you for the snow we got today. It's so beautiful, Lord. Thank you for making me in your image, God. I am wonderfully and fearfully made.

Thank you for the snow this morning, and thank you for the opportunity to serve you by giving all those bagels to the mission. Please be with the people at the mission. Grant the volunteers and staff wisdom, patience and love, and help those who go there to get jobs and be able to afford homes—help them piece their lives together.

You are a magnificent and all-powerful, mighty promise-keeper. Thank you!

Thank you for the warmer temperatures we've been having. Thank you for the three deer I saw this morning. Thank you for my family. Thank you for my friends. Thank you for the beautiful moon I saw tonight.

You are awesome and majestic and almighty and powerful. You are a gentle-shepherd, a mighty warrior, a loving father. Thank you for being so wonderful, and thank you for loving me and protecting me always.

12-23-97 Thank you for Christmas. Thank you for giving up your awesome home in heaven to come and live with a bunch of foul sinners on earth. Thank you for being my Savior.

Her last entry: You are truly an amazing God. You work in mysterious and wonderful ways. You are awesome and majestic. I love you, Lord. In Jesus' name, Amen.

On the bookmark found in her prayer journal are these words from Matthew 22:37:

"You shall love the Lord your God with all your heart; with all your soul, and with all your mind."

About the Author

Ken Hekman is a husband, father, poet, writer, speaker, and international healthcare consultant based in Holland, Michigan. Current information about the author can be found through his website at *www.hekmangroup.com.*

Index